FRAGMENTS OF US

AF664949

SRIVIDYA YELURIPATI'S

BookLeaf Publishing
India | USA | UK

Presentation by *BookLeaf Publishing*

Web: www.bookleafpub.com
E-mail: info@bookleafpub.com

ISBN: 9789369549276

First edition 2025

DEDICATION

To my family, the unwavering foundation of my strength, and to my friends, whose belief in me outshone even my own. Your support has been my guiding light.

CONTENTS

PREFACE

The space between words often holds the truest meaning, just as the silence between moments can speak louder than any action. This collection, *Fragments of Us*, is an exploration of those spaces—the pauses, the unspoken, the contradictions that define us. It is an attempt to capture the fragile balance between love and pain, connection and distance, the quiet ache of growing and the sharp clarity of loss.

At the heart of this book lies the tension between our inner selves and the external world that shapes us. The poems here are fragments of that struggle—tiny glimpses into the heart's deepest desires, its rawest wounds, and its fragile moments of healing. They speak to the complexity of human relationships, from the innocent simplicity of childhood to the tangled mess of adulthood, from the warmth of family to the devastating coldness of betrayal.

Yet, amid the confusion and hurt, there is a constant search for meaning. A search for something that makes sense of it all. These poems do not offer answers, but rather create space for reflection, for feeling, and for understanding that we are all in this together—whether in joy or sorrow, certainty or doubt.

This collection is as much about the journey as it is about the destination. It's about the moments we revisit, the parts of ourselves we piece together, and the uncharted paths we take toward self-discovery. For even in the darkest hours, when we question everything we thought we knew, there is always the possibility of change, of growth, and of finding peace in the fragments of who we once were.

Thank you for letting my words find a home within you.

May these poems invite you to question ,to reflect, and to embrace the complexity of your own journey, serving as a reminder that even with our fractures ,we remain whole.

PART 1

STITCHING THE PAST

1

THE QUIET DISTANCE

With time, what once was love's fierce fight
Turned into silent wars between us.
What changed?
Did I change? Did you?
Where did the effort go,
The tenderness that once defined us?
Now, only echoes remain.

Oh, my love, please trust me—
My love for you is endless,
As long as breath fills my lungs.
But what happened to us?
What turned our battles cold,
Leaving you distant, unmoved?

Where did those eyes go?
The ones that once searched for mine,
Now they turn away,
Avoiding, slipping into shadows,
Veiled behind excuses—
"Work," "Long hours,"
Empty words that feel like walls.

My love, tell me—
Why this distance?
What happened to us?
My heart aches for answers,
Yet I wait,
As time slips quietly by.

2

LOVE DOESN'T HURT THIS MUCH

Why does it hurt when you say you love me?
Why does it sting, even in your words?

Is it because I see the truth now—
That your love was a lie from the start?

If I was such a burden,
Why not just let me go?

I could have walked away long ago,
But you never set me free,
Holding me in this space—neither close nor far,
Just suspended in your silence,
In your empty promises.

I waited, I hoped,
But you never made a choice.

And now, I'm left with one question:
Did you ever love me at all?

3

UNEXPECTED MEETING

You returned,
Like dark clouds creeping across a bright sky,
An uninvited guest,
A reminder of wounds I thought had healed,
Of feelings I thought I'd overcome.

Before you spoke,
I could feel it—the tension,
The unease flooding my veins,
The dread that I couldn't shake.
My heart skipped a beat,
Then quickly pulled itself back together,
Only to feel the sharp sting of your presence.

You were different now—
The youth and vitality you once wore so proudly,
Now faded, worn down by time,
The habits that once soothed you,
Now heavier, dragging you down.

Your heart, once bright,
Now a hollow shade of its former self,
And in your eyes,
I saw the remnants of a man I didn't recognize.

But you returned—
Just when I thought the storm had passed,
Just when I thought I had put the past to rest.
Yet, the storm inside me stirs again—
The old wounds reopen,
But this time, I'm not the same.

4

THE WEIGHT OF LIES

Just as I expected,
You cried,
Pleading for another chance,
Begging me to accept your apology.

Just as I expected,
You found yourself drowning in your own choices,
The weight of your lies,
The friends who once surrounded you—
Now ghosts, just like you left me.

You're left with nothing—
A broken heart,
An empty pocket,
Old age creeping in far too soon.

I saw the spark in your eyes
When you saw me—
This time, you made sure
I believed you had changed.

For a fleeting moment,
I almost did.
But when you tried to waltz back into my life,
I saw you for what you really were—
A shadow of who I thought you could be.

"I forgive you," I said,
But that was for me,
Not for you.

And you,
You weren't allowed back in.
That,
That left you cold to your core.

5

FLEETING MOMENTS

Just when I thought I'd let go,
The real you began to show.
The cracks in your smile,
The eyes that no longer reflected mine.

The old patterns returned—
Cold one moment,
Warm the next.
And every time I mentioned it,
Everything shifted back to "normal,"
A pattern that confused me.

I wanted to believe in the change,
But my heart,
It remained cautious.
You apologized,
But was it enough?

I remember the days when
I was always at fault,
When the plate was turned to my side,
When nothing was ever good enough.

And now, I ask—
How can someone change so completely,
And for how long?

6

A SHADOW OF WHO YOU WERE

I almost believed.
But then, your actions revealed the truth.
You returned with apologies—
Words carefully crafted to sound sincere,
But they were hollow,
Like a song without a melody.

I thought you had changed,
That we could rewrite our story.
But you showed me otherwise.
It wasn't love you sought,
It was control—
To feed off my energy,
To regain what you lost.

For a moment, I believed you,
Enough to let you in—
Only to be stabbed again.
Your words,
A dagger disguised as an apology.

No.
You won't rewrite my story.
Not this time.

I see you now for what you are,
And I'll walk away—
For the last time.

7

NEVER ENOUGH

I crossed oceans for you,
Yet here I stand—unseen,
My love, a burden you never asked for. "A burden you wanted to get rid of "

I bent every rule,
Pushed beyond every limit,
For a smile,
For a glimmer of recognition.
Yet I remain a ghost in your world,
Yearning for the warmth that never came.

Your words,
"I love you,"
But where are the actions?
They echo in an empty room,
Hollow and distant.

I gave all that I am,
Yet still,
I am alone.
Not because you're absent,
But because your heart was never really there.

Perhaps I was never meant to be enough—
A passing moment,
A fleeting thought,
While you were always somewhere else.

I gave everything,
And still,
I was never enough.

8

LOVE, FOR ONCE BE HONEST

Love,
Was it only me who tried so hard,
For all these years, for all these scars?
Be honest, just once,
Why did you choose me, when you never really wanted me?
Yet still, you stayed.

Love,
For once, be honest—
What did I do to deserve this?
Was I your muse, or just a pawn,
In a game I never knew?

Love,
For once, be honest.
Stop hiding behind empty promises,
And tell me the truth.

9

AM I NOT CLOSE ENOUGH?

Am I not close enough to share your joys and fears?
Then what am I, to share the most intimate parts of my life?
Why am I not a part of yours,
When you are my whole world?

Was I not close enough to notice when you were struggling?
Then what am I,
But someone you call when it's convenient,
When it's easy?

Was I not close enough to ask for your time?
Then what am I?

Oh, my love,
I spent all my days and nights thinking of you,
Always by your side.
Then why,
In this moment of need,
Am I left alone?

Am I not close enough?

10

DARLING, WHERE DID IT GO?

Darling,
Where did the promises go?
The ones to never leave, to build a future together?

Darling,
Where did the conversations go?
From dawn to dusk, no silence between us,
Now nothing but quiet,
A distance I can't cross.

Darling,
Where did the person I met go?
The one who felt like home,
The one who looked at me with love?

Darling,
I don't know the person standing before me now.
Tell me, who are you?
The one who promised me forever,
Or the stranger I don't recognize?

Darling,
I feel lost, confused.
What changed along the way?
Was it me? Was it you? Or was it us?

Is this the end?
Or just the beginning of something unforeseen?

11

DEAR, THE WAY YOU LEFT

Dear,
The way you left,
Left me with nothing but silence.

Dear,
The way you left,
Made me see my love for you,
And the truth of your intentions.

Dear,
The way you left,
Made me realize that even the longest relationships can end.
It's not the time that matters,
But the love that was never truly there.

Dear,
The way you left,
Taught me that feelings unreciprocated
Can break you.
I was never your destination,
Just a passing stop,
A muse,
Not a love to stay.

Dear,
The way you left,
Showed me how blind I was,
Facing away from reality,
Believing in something that was never true.

Dear,
The way you left,
Left me with nothing but echoes—
Of love unreturned,
Of trust broken.

At last,
I understood why you entered my life,
And why you had to leave.

12

OH, MY FATE

Oh, my fate,
Even after how you betrayed me,
I kept waiting for you.

Am I addicted to you?
Or is my love so deep,
That I can't escape,
Even after all you did?

Oh, my fate,
You moved on—
Like nothing ever mattered.
How could you forget what once was everything?
Was it ever anything at all?

Oh, my fate,
I hate this feeling—
The way I'm still stuck,
Not sure if I'm trapped,
Or if I've been living in your absence,
Avoiding the truth I can't face.

Oh, my fate,
What is this I'm doing?
Is falling out of love so hard?
Then how did you move on so easily?

Oh, my fate,
Was it even love for you?
Or was I just a fleeting dream,
A shadow in your life?

13

EMPTY CHAIR

There's an empty chair by the window,
Where you once sat,
With your smile, your laughter,
Your gentle presence.

I wonder if you still remember,
The way we shared dreams in the quiet of the night.
Now, it's just me,
Staring at that vacant chair,
Wishing you'd come back,
But knowing you never will.

I fill the silence with thoughts of you,
But nothing fills the space,
Nothing heals the ache.

The chair remains,
Empty and still,
Just like the parts of me you took
When you walked away.

14

THE GHOST OF US

Sometimes, I feel like I'm haunted,
By the ghost of us.
It lingers in the air,
In every corner of the house,
In the space where our love once thrived.

You're gone,
But the echoes of your voice,
The warmth of your touch,
Still haunt my every thought.

I keep chasing shadows,
Trying to bring back something
That was never meant to stay.

I've learned to live with the ghost,
But it never leaves,
Just like the memories of you.

15

A LAST GOODBYE

I don't know how to say goodbye,
To something I once thought would last forever.
Do I speak the words,
Or let them fade away,
Like the love we once shared?

I never imagined it would end this way,
With no closure,
No resolution,
Just silence.

But here we are,
At the end of something beautiful,
Now broken,
Now lost.

Goodbye, my love,
Goodbye,
Though I never wanted to say it.

16

THE END OF THE ROAD

We walked this road together,
But somewhere along the way,
You stopped walking beside me.

The path we once shared is now empty,
A trail I'm left to follow alone.

I don't know when it all fell apart,
When the love we had turned to dust.
But here I am,
At the end of the road,
With no one to turn to,
No one to share the journey.

I've reached the end,
And now I see—
The road wasn't meant to last.
Maybe it was never really ours.

17

YOUR NAME

Your name still lingers on my lips,
A bitter taste,
A reminder of what I lost.

I whisper it in the dark,
Hoping to call you back,
But you're gone,
And you're never coming back.

I say your name,
But it no longer holds the same meaning.
It's just a word now,
A shadow of the love we shared.

Your name doesn't bring me comfort anymore.
It only brings pain.
I'll say it one last time,
And then I'll let it go.

18

WHY DO I STILL WAIT?

I don't know why I still wait,
For someone who doesn't care.
For someone who has forgotten me.

I know I should move on,
I know I should let go,
But something keeps me holding on.

I keep waiting,
For a call that never comes,
For a message that won't be sent.

I keep hoping,
For a love that's already gone,
For a heart that's already moved on.

Why do I still wait?
Is it love, or just the hope of what could've been?

19

WHAT'S LEFT?

What's left when love fades away?
When promises break and the trust shatters?

What's left when the words turn to lies,
And the memories turn to dust?

What's left when you leave,
And I'm left to pick up the pieces?

What's left is a heart that's broken,
But still beating.
A soul that's scarred,
But still searching for light.

What's left is me,
Trying to heal,
Trying to move forward,
Even though I don't know how.

20

UNSPOKEN WORDS

There are words I never said,
Words I kept locked away,
Afraid they'd be too much for you to hear.

I wanted to tell you how much I loved you,
How much you meant to me.
But the words always got caught in my throat,
Stuck in a place where they couldn't break free.

Now, those words are just silence,
Unspoken and lost.
Regret lingers where love once lived,
And I wonder if you ever knew.

21

THE SPACE YOU LEFT BEHIND

The space you left behind is still here,
In every corner of this room,
In every moment we shared.

I try to fill it with distractions,
With things to keep my mind busy,
But nothing fills the void,
Nothing replaces you.

I never thought I'd be here,
Staring at the emptiness,
Wishing for something I can't have.

The space you left behind is all I have now,
A constant reminder of what I lost.

22

ONCE, WE WERE EVERYTHING

Once, we were everything—
Two hearts beating as one,
Two souls intertwined,
With promises of forever.

But forever never came.
And now, we're nothing.

I hold onto the memories,
The moments when we were in sync,
When love felt like the only truth.

But now, I wonder—
Was it ever real?
Or just a dream I made up,
A fantasy that couldn't last?

Once, we were everything.
Now, we are nothing.

23

A HEART STILL LOVES YOU

A heart still loves you,
Even after you walked away.
Even after the hurt, the pain, the tears.

A heart still loves you,
Though it knows you've moved on,
Though it knows you've let go.

A heart still loves you,
Because love doesn't just vanish.
It stays, even when it's not wanted.

A heart still loves you,
But it's learning to let go.
It's learning to love itself again.

24

WHEN YOU LEFT ME

When you left,
A part of me left too.
I miss the little Miss I used to be.
But it's the nature of love—
To find, break, and rebuild.

So here I am,
Picking up the pieces once more,
Reclaiming my identity,
Starting anew,
As the woman I was always meant to be.

25

I HAVE LOVED YOU FOREVER

I have loved you for as long as I can remember,
And still, I do—
But do you love me, too?
That question stings,
A shadow that lingers in my heart.

My love,
Why won't you say what's wrong?
Can't we talk,
Make changes,
And find our way back?

I've always loved you,
And I always will,
No matter your flaws or imperfections.
I love you with everything I have,
Exactly as you are.

26

WHAT IF

I always think,
What if our love was perfect?
Not perfect like in stories or dramas,
But perfect as it was—

The fights, the forgiveness, the growth.
What if everything aligned?
What if we were still together?
What a life that could have been.

27

WE LOVED EACH OTHER

We loved each other with all of ourselves,
My heart bleeds with the silence between us,
It hurts to accept the distance.

But what can we do?
Not even gods can change destiny.
Life happened,
Love deepened,
And our souls took different paths.

28

THE ILLUSION OF WORTH

We know.
We know we're being used,
We see through the shades of smiles.

The plots disguised as love,
Highlighting patterns we can't ignore,
Yet we refuse to see.

Is it love?
Or the fear of losing them?
What is it, really?

Then why do we run after those who avoid us?
Why do we crave attention,
From those who barely notice?

Can't we see we're being used,
Chasing what's never truly ours?

Why do we seek validation,
From hearts that remain distant?
Is it just a fleeting hunger,
For a worth defined by their gaze?

29

"THE WEIGHT SHE CARRIES"

What can she say,
When she always hides her face—
The blemishes, the chin hair,
The stubborn weight that won't disappear.

The constant exhaustion
That no one seems to understand,
The mood swings, the aches, the cramps,
All with no one to lend a hand.

What can she say
When they tell her, "It's just PCOS—
You can manage it!"
She wishes she could,
But with the weight of expectations
Pressing her down,
Even the smallest task feels like drowning.

People are immersed in
Perfect skin, perfect hair,
Unrealistic expectations,
Pointing out every flaw they can see—
Even the ones they themselves are hiding.

She longs for a world to change,
Where understanding, not shame, is embraced.

30

"I WOKE UP"

I have slept many days,
In the hope of waking to a different dawn.

But each day, I woke up
To the pain that lingered,
Longer than before.

Who said only a weapon can bruise or kill?
Have you ever been hurt by words—
Words from those who should protect you?

I slept beneath a white coating,
Hidden from the words,
Thinking they'd disappear
If I surrendered more.

Do they?

I slept in the ignorance of
Being loyal to an unworthy foe,
Who only abused my love.

I woke up.
I finally woke up to the harsh truth—
There isn't any love.

31

"SCATTERED PIECES"

You found me in peace,
You found me in love—
The laughter, the big bright eyes,
Long hair flowing like a river.

You found me in serenity,
Only to shatter me into pieces.
The big bright eyes that once saw the world in color,
Now see it in black and white.

The eyes that once smiled beyond the lips,
Now hold stories unsaid.
The eyes that never knew betrayal,
Now soaked in tears of hurt.

The long hair, cut short—
Each strand a memory,
Tied to the past
I picked up the shattered pieces.

You showed up, seemed to help,
But scattered me a bit more.

Didn't you feel my pain?
Or do you enjoy my suffering?

32

"DID YOU FEEL MY LOVE?"

Did you feel my love?
Or did you feel nothing at all?
For I can't make sense of your words and actions.

I felt it in every bone,
What you were doing—
But I kept quiet,
Hoping it would last just a little longer.

I sensed the betrayal
Before it even showed its face,
But I chose to focus on hope,
Ignoring the signs that whispered the truth.

I wish I had spoken up
When things were still messy—
I could have walked away then,
And lived a life in peace.

33

THE MOMENT SHE LEFT

I saw her leaving,
From the car, from my life,
I watched her fade in the rearview mirror.

In the pouring rain,
The glass reflecting a distorted image of her.

My eyes teared up,
Unable to see her clearly—
Is it my eyes, or the mirror?

I could've stopped her,
But if I did,
I wouldn't have answers to the questions
She needed me to answer.

Only after she left,
Did I realize what she truly meant to me—
What I lost.

34

WHY FEW THINGS ARE LEFT UNSAID?

I know you would come,
You'd come back running,
If I called and said,
"I don't want to go."

I know you'd pick me up,
With all the happiness and excitement.

I saw your face when I was leaving,
Your smile fading,
Your eyes speaking
What your lips didn't.

Our last-minute conversation
Was nothing but silence.
You wished I didn't leave,
But you didn't stop me, either.

Why are some things left unsaid?

35

"THE LAST CALL"

Neither of us knew
That it would be the last time
We'd see each other.
If I had known, I would never
Have ended the call.

I wish I had let him say
What he needed to.

I wish that day hadn't come,
When we spoke for the last time.

I wish I could travel back,
To say a few things,
To hear a few more.
Or maybe—
To stop myself from saying anything,
To leave it at a simple "hi,"
Or not even that.

The guilt, the fear of never seeing him again,
It's so heavy,
Growing heavier each day.

I wish that ending never came.

36

WRONG TIME, RIGHT PEOPLE

I saw tears in your eyes,
Like never before.

You broke down
When I left.
I could see the pain,
The struggle.

But I'm helpless, love,
When things were in your control,
You played.
When everything changed,
You changed too,
But at the wrong time.

Just like
Wrong time, right people,
Right people, wrong time.

I wish things were
Different.

37

IF ONLY YOU COULD SEE

If only you could see my success,
I know you're wishing me luck,
Sending me angels
From the other side.

But—
What success is it,
When I can't celebrate it with you?
What fame is it,
When you're not a part of it?
What luxury is it,
When I can't share it with you?

I know,
I know it's all your love
And luck you're showering on me.
I know you're watching me
From afar—
If only I could see you too,
My pain would ease a bit.

38

OUR INCOMPLETE STORY

Our story, incomplete,
Ended without an ending.
The quiet that follows
When I think of you,
And realize I haven't moved on,
Not as much as I thought I had.

It feels like an eternity has passed without you,
Yet I still wonder how you are,
Though I'm no longer a part of your life.

Or maybe—
I never was.

My heart bleeds each time I see
The same shirt you wore,
The watch, the song you used to sing—
It still echoes in my ears.

It's not easy to unlove someone you once loved.
Maybe moving on is
Realizing you're no longer part of their world,
That they've learned to live without you,
And learning, too, to live your life without them.

PART 2

WHERE LOVE LIVES

39

LITTLE DID I KNOW

Little did I know,
You would stay forever—
A soul sister,
Keeping our bond alive
Across the distance,
Even when we're far apart.

We shared every little detail,
No moment is too small to miss.
Nobody could ever replace your place,
My sweet pie, my confidante.

Who says sisters are bound by blood?
We've proven them wrong,
Our families wove a bond
One that will last for eternity.

40

THE ROAD TRIP

The road trip, a miracle came true,
Amidst our busy schedules,
We made it.
We kept our promise,
To meet again.

Some with the love of their lives,
Others are pet parents,
Journeying with their furry friends,
The longing finally ended
On a quiet evening,
Gazing at the moonlight.

We talked all night,
Promising to never leave each other,
And to reunite.

41

BOUND BY RESPECT

The love we shared, envied by others,
Always under scrutiny,
Seeking faults,
But to no avail.

Little did they know,
We respected each other
More than love itself.
Our friendship grew so strong,
Becoming the foundation of our bond.

For the respect
You show me—and all women—
Made me love you
Even more.

It takes respect, nurturing,
And gentleness to weave a relationship,
To bind us together as one.

42

HOW DO YOU UNDERSTAND ME SO MUCH?

How do you understand me so much,
Even when words fail?

The pain, the love,
The happiness?

It feels like you heal my soul,
Though you never broke it.
Everything seems possible with you,
Every problem fades away
As you walk in.

My strength, my love,
My friend, my forever.
You healed me.
You brought the softness in me to light.

43

A LOVE LIKE NO OTHER

I felt so happy
When your mom came by,
Looked into your eyes,
And said, "I'm proud of you."

You broke every chain
That was holding me back,
You walked behind me
And let me take the lead.

Today, I choose to be
Behind you,
Beside you,
In every thick and thin.
I choose to trust you,
Your decisions.

Though they didn't say it,
The women in the room
Felt both happy and sad—
Happy, that I could take the lead,
Sad, they couldn't achieve their aim.

I wish every woman could have
A love like you,
One that allows
Her femininity to flow and glow.
A love that nurtures,
Respects, and uplifts,
A love that becomes her strength
And her soft place to fall.

44

HAPPY ENDING

What is a happy ending—
A career well-earned?
A family, children, and home?

Or is it the promise
To never give up on each other,
To stand together through thick and thin?

Supporting each other's dreams,
Respecting boundaries,
Staying loyal,
Finding solace in one another?

Feminine energy—
A mother's touch,
It rises when she lets her softness bloom,
Without the need to fight,
Without the pressure to be seen or heard.

A happy ending is found in understanding,
In love that nurtures and lets us be.

45

THE LOST ERA OF LOVE

I'm stuck in the era of
Handwritten letters,
Holding hands while crossing the road,
Gifting handmade tokens of love.

Old movies on a winter night,
Tucked in a blanket,
Laughing together at the humor,
Living fully in the moment,
And making memories that last.

What was I searching for in
The new era,
The digital age of love?
Fancy gifts, yet no trace of heart,
Pride overshadowing what once was pure.

Does my kind of love still exist?

46

FAIRY LIGHTS

The fairy lights
We bring,
Every Diwali, every celebration,

The strings of lights
That brightens our smiles,
Letting our eyes sparkle,

Spreading light
To every corner of the house.

But do those who give the light,
Ever find brightness
In their own lives?
Or are they lost
In the process of making others' lives beautiful?

47

"TO MY PARENTS"

Hey, Mom and Dad,
I'm writing this as I take to the skies,
Soaring high, spreading my wings,
Building an empire.

An empire worthy of you both,
Worthy of your sacrifices—
Sending me far away,
With heavy hearts, constant thoughts,
How will I manage?

But I promise,
I'll never let go
Of this opportunity.
I'll hold it close and make it mine.

Up here, I can't see the ground,
Only the limitless sky,
The bright sun,
And the white clouds,
Like the opportunities ahead—
The future I'll build,
The path I'll walk,
With your blessings.

I'm not scared, Mom and Dad,
For I trust in my wings,
And the strength of your wishes.

I promise to return,
As an empress.

48

GIFTS FROM PARENTS

The gifts parents give,
To surprise their children,
Even when they've grown up.

The handmade treasures,
The flowers we love,
The fruits we savor,
The delights that bring us joy.

Good morning greetings,
Even when they're drowned in their own worries.
The festival blessings,
Unmatched by a hundred other wishes.

Always behind us,
Always protecting us,
No matter how far we've come.

49

WHEN WE MET AGAIN

We met after a long, long time.
I thought of you throughout the journey,
Each station bringing the joy of closing the distance.

Finally, we met.
You wished to see me
First thing when you woke up,
And there I was,
Right in front of you.

You grinned at your own stubbornness,
Smiling from ear to ear,
Walking through the room,
Finding excuses to tease, help, or talk.

The quiet moments shared were always precious—
No name,
No label,
Just pure bliss.

50

GOODBYE FOR THIS LIFETIME

I wish I had said,
When we were together,
How much you mean to me.
How much I love you.

Of course, I never spoke it aloud in words,
But—
I always conveyed it through my actions,
And you understood.

You understood like no other—
My love, my smile, my pain.

I regret not being verbal,
So I could see your brightest, most beautiful smile,
Just one more time.

I regret you being far away,
With no hope of meeting.

I never got enough time
To say a proper goodbye.

If ever another world exists,
We'll meet there,
Without the constraints of time.

Goodbye for this lifetime,
Till we meet again.

51

CONVEY MY LOVE

Oh, time of love!
Convey my sweetheart—
I have always been in love.

Convey that I loved him,
And will continue to.

Convey my yearning,
Convey my suffering.

Convey to end this
Separation,
Convey to return,
For there is a person
Who waits with hope in their eyes
And love in their heart.

52

BENEATH SHARED SKIES

We are separated by destiny,
But united by the same sunsets, no matter the miles between.

No matter where we go,
The moon follows us both.

The stars sparkle the same,
The wind that blows
Reminds me,
We are under the same sky, at least.

53

"TO YOU, MY GUIDING LIGHT"

A brother,
A friend,
Or perhaps more of a well-wisher?
Who knew you would come to mean so much?

Your guidance,
Your words of strength,
And the banter we share that fills our chats with laughter,
Creating lasting memories for years to come.

With every passing moment,
Our bond only grows deeper,
Stronger,
Unbreakable.

54

"THE SISTER'S ROAR"

I know, if I told my sister
Half the traumas I've had,
She'd drown the mountains for me.

I know, if I showed her
The people who betrayed and belittled me,
She'd break hell loose on them,
No mercy, no hesitation.

I know, if I asked her anything,
At any time,
She would never deny.
She'd drop everything to be my aid,
Without a second thought.

I know my sister,
Raising me like her own baby.
I've felt her love like a second mother's,
A mother who's as fierce as a lion,
When it comes to her baby sister.

55

A SOLO DATE

As I sat by the coffee table,
On a solo date,
I tucked myself in my warmer,
A harsh winter.

Slowly sipping my coffee,
Reading a book,
Suddenly, I caught you looking at me.

Caught in the act, you—
Scared and alerted,
Turned your gaze to the window.

Then came my sweet pie,
Surprised to see you there,
And introduced us.
You gently whispered,
"I'm sorry, I thought I saw you."

Which I suppose you did,
From her profile.

PART 3

TIMELESS TRUTHS

56

THE ERA OF INNOCENCE

Childhood was all fun and games
Gathering friends and playing under a tree,
The never-ending chit-chats.

From entering the classroom
Till going home,
A bond we shared in school
Didn't stop just at school.

We continued till late evenings,
Sundays, every festival we were together.

Wishing and twirling around in new clothes,
Sharing sweets,
A little gossip, jealousy when
You got friendly with the new kid
The era of innocence.

57

THE END OF AN ERA

But then, all at once,
It ended.
The games stopped,
The laughter faded.

Everybody moved on,
The roads we roamed seem
Lifeless now,
Our shuttle bats hung
By the door,
Dust settling,
Since I'm left alone, without my companion.

Each of us carrying a piece of that time—
The end of an era.

58

THE QUIET WE SHARED

I miss the quiet we shared,
Before everything changed.
Before words became weapons,
And silence turned to sorrow.

I miss the way we could be together,
Without needing to speak.
The comfort of your presence,
The peace of just being near you.

Now, silence is all we have,
But it's a cold kind of quiet.
A silence that says more than words ever could.

I miss the quiet we shared—
When love was all we needed.

59

EVEN AFTER YOU LEFT

Even after you left,
A part of you remains with me,
A part of me is still with you.
The café stands as a witness,
To what once was, and to what we were.

A memory of you lingers in my mind,
Despite knowing there's no future for us.
I let the thoughts be,
And return to my daily routine.

60

THE PAST THAT WANDERS

The past still lingers around me,
Like a familiar face,
With a dark history,
Making me question my actions.

Though I want to let go,
It stays—
Not as a burden,
But as a lesson,
A reminder for when I fumble.

61

TIMELESS TRUTHS

Time is cruel, isn't it?
It is faithful only to
Raw emotions—
Love, betrayal, redemption,
Loyalty,
And nature.

We are lost in time,
Fighting to hold on to
Emotions and feelings,
Caught in the tide of passing moments.
Time does not wait for us.

But maybe that is the beauty of time—
It only makes the unwavering things
Timeless.

Beauty fades,
Charm hides,
The spring of youth
Becomes winter.
But our loyalty shines,
Undiminished by time's trail.

We've lost, and we've won,
But in the end,
Is time cruel?
Or is it the measure of all we endure?

62

THE BATTLE WITHIN

Memories fade,
Tears no longer fall,
Like a soldier, faithful and still,
Holding on, waiting for the command to rise—
Will I ever command?

Memories fade,
But what of scars?
Do they fade too?
Or do they carry stories
Of battles fought and won,
Where we stood as warriors,
Fighting time's cruel march,
In the timeless war against forgetting?

63

WHAT IS BEAUTY?

What is beauty?
Does it lie in the golden age of youth?
Lustrous locks of hair,
Painted nails,
Or those lovely eyes?

Is it in the masculine power,
Or feminine softness?

Is it in a wallet filled with pride,
Buying a drink,
Or paying the bill—
Chasing fleeting pleasures?

Or is it waking up beside the one
You love,
In your '60s,
With white hairs replacing
The grey shades,
Wrinkles from endless smiles,
Helping to make coffee
In your twilight years?

The spring of old age
Takes the place of beauty.

64

FRESH MEMORIES

I was at the balcony,
Gazing at the sky.
The new place took
Time to adjust,

But you made me feel at home.
You closed my eyes from behind,
The warmth of your hands—
I can still feel it,
Whenever I remember.

The first coffee you made,
For us,
The first star-gazing,
The long conversations,
The first gift you brought me.

Everything feels so fresh,
Even after years,
The cool morning breeze,
And your coffee.

65

YOUR EYES, THEIR MAGIC

Years have passed,
But I still can't forget you.

I remember—
Your words,
Your smile,
Your style,
Everything.

Whenever I see anyone
Resembling your words or style,
My heart drifts back to you.

Your eyes always spoke,
Even when you were quiet.
Always hopeful,
Always soft in their gaze.

I haven't seen such
Softened eyes
Since then—
Truly magical,
Truly peaceful.

66

BETWEEN HEART AND TIME

My eyes dried up, crying for you,
Still hopelessly waiting for you.

They don't know—
They can never see you.
If they could,
They would never blink before you.

Oh, my love!
What kind of battle is this?
Is it within—failing to control my heart?

Or
Against time?

PART 4

WHISPERS OF LIFE

67

"THE PRICE OF HER DREAMS"

The life of every woman—
Some are blessed with
The love of two families after marriage,
While others face taunts,
Comparisons,
Favoritism,
And the endless cycle of
Working vs. Non-working.

When they try to build their dreams,
They are labeled.

We teach them to be competitive,
Obedient, and calm,
We give them the hope of the sky,
Then clip their wings
When they try to fly.

When will we stop blaming her?
Are we truly doing justice?

Give her the love and respect she deserves,
Let her dreams soar,
And you will witness
The most powerful feminine energy
You've ever known.

68

PRIDE OF A FALLING STAR

How proud must a falling star
Feel,
Even while it's descending?

It sparks a light
In millions of hearts,
Each wishing on its glow,
Clinging to hope.

Very few are given the chance
To uplift others
Even while they are falling.

Like a soldier,
Proud in the fight,
Kissing the earth before the final sleep,
Fighting for a cause greater than themselves.

69

"THE BURDEN OF UNSPOKEN DREAMS"

The struggle of a young man
Often goes unseen.
He's not thanked for his sacrifices,
For everything he does for his family—
It's just his responsibility.

What if he ever spoke
Of his own wishes,
Of the dreams he longs to achieve?
Could the elder son ever spread his wings,
Ever soar high enough to reach them?

The sacrifices he makes,
The weight of watching his parents grow old,
The responsibility of younger siblings,
The comparisons from relatives—
What must he go through,
Every single day?

The boy who dreamt of singing
Now sings only on his way to work,
The work that barely pays the bills.
If only he could pursue his passion,
He might live the life he dreamt,
Instead of living in the shadows of expectations.

70

"THE REALITY OF RELATIONSHIPS"

Relationships aren't one-time things,
They're forever and beyond.

In a world rampant with fast culture,
We've forgotten that we can repair things
Before they become irreparable.

Just like relationships need normalcy,
They need honesty, reality, support, and understanding.

We can't be happy every single day,
Life is a journey of ups and downs,
Like walking through a tunnel,
Not knowing where it ends.
But we can take the next step, carefully,
With the torch of hope in hand.

In relationships, we must carry that torch—
Of understanding, empathy, and sticking to reality.

Life is meant to be lived in peace,
But peace often feels boring.
We think we're not happy like others,
And start picking unnecessary fights.

The dreams are not the problem,
rather it's the dream of always being happy,
Without acknowledging life's unexpected turns.

71

"THE WORLD DOESN'T WORK YOUR WAY"

Be mindful of the words you speak.
Many have stopped dressing the way they once did,
Many have stopped wearing the big goggles they loved,
Many have stopped taking pictures,
Many have stopped singing.

Even more have stopped showing up to parties,
Feeling like odd ducks,
Unable to fit into the world.

Let people be.
Let them live.
The world doesn't work according to your wishes.

You might think fast fashion is everything,
For them,
Old money is everything,
Vintage is love.

For you,
It's all about aesthetic pictures.
For them,
It's about capturing memories—
No filters,
No makeup,
Just living in the moment.

For you,
It's perfectionism.
For them,
It's mindfulness—
Living each day,
As it comes.

72

"DESTINY'S PLAN"

Destiny is planned for everyone,
According to their need.

Some deserve the sun—
The golden hue,
The garden with flowers,
Sunkissed lives,
Radiant and warm.

Some deserve the rain—
The dark skies surrounding,
The gusty winds,
Pouring rain to calm the soul,
A peaceful embrace from the heavens.

73

A CALL FOR CONSIDERATION

I wish people could learn to be considerate,
To understand what others are going through.

Not everything is seen,
Not everything is visible to the human eye.

The pain one withholds
Burdening the soul,
Let the moment pass—
Give them time to heal and come through it.

If not for empathy,
At least be quiet.
Offer them support and strength,
Not another battle they have to fight.

Let the world rest in peace,
In understanding, in silence, in care.

74

INTROVERTED TRANQUILITY

Who said an introverted life is boring?
It's the tranquility they live with.

They aren't detached from people—
They're simply mindful of their life.

They finish their work,
Return home,
Play the music they love,
Create a cozy space.

Finish their favorite book,
A series, or art—
Anything that feeds their soul.

They savor the silence,
The rain,
The wind gusts,
A serene, quiet, dark night—
Their way of unwinding.

It's beautiful,
In its own way.

75

THE WARRIOR IN HER

The girl swirled in a beautiful pista green half saree,
Braided her hair with jasmine,
The golden hue made her glow
Like an angel on earth,
Radiating warmth,
As if she were a living miracle.

The Alta on her feet,
A deep red,
Her laughter filled the space
Like soft music,
Light and pure.

Everyone turned to see,
The enchantress—
Her anklets echoing,
The sound lingering in the air,
Even the flowers seemed to envy
Her beauty.

Just when I was admiring her beauty,
She unfolded her warrior form—
Fighting the bull,
As ferocious as a mother defending her child,
She fought even without knowing the kid.
While many stood, confused and scared,
She took the girl in her embrace,
Slowly wiping away the tears of fear.

Her eyes, once innocent,
Now fierce as the red of her Alta feet,
Shifting from innocence to envisioning the threat,
Hoping to save,
The sweaty face gave an impression—
She could be a beauty,
She could be a warrior.

I salute her.

76

COMPANION IN THE VALLEY

I was surrounded by a vast valley of mountains,
The lush greenery stretched, a carpet on the floor,
The moist soil beneath, a soft embrace,
I felt the grass blades brushing my bare feet.

I walked along the winding path,
A deer appeared, calm and still,
It seemed to guide me, leading the way,
In this peaceful, quiet sway.

Tired and sweaty, I sat by a giant tree,
Its branches waved,
Gently wiping my sweat with the cool breeze.
With my long companion beside me, I drifted to sleep.

77

THE MYSTICAL FOREST

The mystical forest,
Surrounded by sky-reaching trees,
The darkness swallowed the daylight.
I was navigating my way out,
To no avail,
Scared, looking here and there,
The soft touch of creeper leaves
Felt like a snake.
Walking slowly,
I ventured deeper into the woods.

I was flabbergasted by the view I saw
At the end of the forest lane—
The mountain top,
The sunlight hit my face,
Its warmth felt like a reassuring pat on a journey uncertain.
The peak view was an achievement indeed.
The waterfall looked like a long stream of milk,
Pouring from the sky.

78

KIDS NOTICE

Kids notice.
They notice the difference in how they're treated.
They remember.
Years might pass, but they still remember.
It makes them question:
What did I do?
Was I not wanted?
What did I do wrong?
They grow up with these questions.

79

THE MAGIC OF LETTERS

The magic of letters has been long lost,
With our elders,
The way a letter conveyed everything,
Even when miles stretched between hearts.
A letter filled the eyes with hope,
And the soul with love.

How can I write those raw emotions now?
The innocent love that time has modified,
Replaced by the fanciest gifts.

Will I still be able to write,
With the same depth,
The same truth,
That once lived in those words?

80

A FATHER'S STRUGGLE

A father's struggle is often forgotten,
Left unseen.

A father also needs new shoes,
But wears the worn-out ones,
Dragging them just a little longer.

He could use private transport,
But chooses the struggle of hanging by the door,
To make ends meet.

Who knows what he's facing outside?
Who knows he's bullied, just like us?

He never shows it,
Always smiles,
Lifting our spirits,
Telling us to take it easy.

Do we understand?
Instead, we say:
"You don't understand. If you could,
You would have brought what I asked."

Doesn't he understand?
He does—
More than anyone.
He faces the world,
Even when branded a failure
By family,
Colleagues,
Friends,
Relatives.

Insults often come disguised as jokes,
And a father takes them with a smile,
Without a word.

Why can't we see the pain behind the smiles?

81

THE UNPAID MOTHER

Isn't it hurtful to read?
A mother, unpaid,
Isn't it painful to see?

A mother,
Often left behind when decisions are made.
Yes, it still happens.

A mother,
Never truly appreciated for the efforts she makes
To keep the family together.

Cooking, feeding, cleaning—
Always working,
Always available.
She can never say no.
And if she does,
The eyes of every family member pop out:
"What were you doing anyway?"
"You stay at home—what's the problem?"

A mother,
Learning smartphones,
Made to feel dumb
For not understanding the ever-changing technology,
For not upgrading herself.

For not dressing up—
Doesn't she wish to?
Who wants to feel invisible,
Wearing old clothes just to avoid damage?

She too deserves a break—
Not just rest, but respect.
A mother's worth is not measured by what she does,
But by the love she gives.

Listen to the unspoken feelings of your mother.

PART 5

ODE TO MYSELF

82

I CHOOSE MYSELF

I love you,
But not more than I love myself.
At least, not anymore.

I kept you as my priority,
When to you, I was just an option.

But now,
I choose myself.
I choose my sleep, my peace,
My self-respect, and my boundaries.

I choose what I deserve,
Not what dazzles me.
I choose the love I never had to fight for—
A love that comes with ease,
And gives without expectations.

From now on,
I am my priority.
No one else will come first but me.

83

AFTER THE STORM

After the storm,
The world is quiet,
But it's not the same.

The winds have passed,
The rain has soaked the earth,
But the damage remains.

I look at the aftermath,
At the broken pieces of what we were,
And
I wonder—
Can anything truly grow from this?

The storm has left me shaken,
But it's also left me stronger.
I'll rebuild,
Piece by piece,
Even if the foundation is cracked.

The storm may have taken you,
But it didn't take my will to survive.

84

LEARNING TO BREATHE AGAIN

I'm learning to breathe again,
Without you by my side.
It's hard, but I'm trying.

I'm learning to stand on my own,
To find strength in places I never knew existed.

I'm learning to love myself,
To forgive myself for loving you so much.

It's a slow process,
But with every breath,
I'm finding my way back to me.

One day, I'll breathe without the weight of you,
And it will feel like freedom.

85

FREEDOM IN LETTING GO

I felt freedom in letting go—
Letting go of what wasn't peaceful,
Of forcing you to be with me,
Of begging you to love me.

Freedom came when I stopped questioning,
When I stopped settling for less.
I stopped looking outside,
And started loving myself.

86

I HAVE CHANGED

I have changed,
The little Miss inside me has changed.
Things that once excited me now hardly bring a smile.

The laughter we shared is now a distant memory,
But for the lessons I've learned,
I'm grateful to start anew,
With all the experiences life has thrown my way.

87

BEAUTY IN BROKENNESS

I see the beauty in broken things now.
The broken crayons still color the same—
Just like people.
They're cracked, shaken, shattered—
Yet they're beautiful.

I found the courage
To begin again,
To embrace life with all its highs and lows,
Loving, respecting, being kind.
Living life to the fullest,
Because the broken souls are colorful,
We just need to see it.

88

THE HEALING MORNINGS

The mornings have become my favorite part of the day.
When the rays of light touch everything softly,
And the air feels different—
Like it's offering something new,
Something I couldn't see before.

I've learned to wake up,
Not just from sleep,
But from everything that weighed me down.

There's a quiet peace
In the way the world begins again.
And I wonder,
Maybe that's how healing works—
Not in grand moments,
But in the simple ones.

89

FROSTED WINDOW

The window covered by the frost,
With pouring rain,
Raindrops slowly ran down my window,
Tracing paths, just like my pain.

I sit beside the glass, and wait,
As love begins to drift away,
For sometimes, letting go of what we hold
Can ease the heart's endless fray.

The subtle sounds of falling rain,
Tripping softly on my windowpane,
Flowing down like fleeting thoughts,
Mimicking my heart's quiet refrain.

90

SUN AND RAIN

I have seen the sun,
I have seen the rain.

The brighter the days,
The higher the pride within me.

The coldest nights,
The darkest hours,
Teach the most powerful lessons—
On loyalty, on love.

We identify our people,
And the pretenders too.

The rain helped me grow
Beyond what I could have ever imagined.
Then I realized—
For a flower to bloom,
Both the rain and the sun are needed.

91

THE FLOWER'S DANCE

The flower on the highest branch
Dances with the wind,
Unbothered by the thought of falling.
With every gust,
It dances a little more,
Enjoying life to the fullest.

Its trust is not in the branch
That holds it,
Nor in the tree
That's rooted deep,
Waiting to be plucked.

The flower trusts itself.
The beauty is within—
Whether it's on the highest branch
Or kissing the ground,
It remains unbothered,
Knowing nothing changes its worth.

92

THE GREATEST ACHIEVEMENT

Somebody asked me,
"What is your biggest achievement?"

I replied, "Myself,"
A secret monologue whispered inside.

After facing harsh realities,
A betrayed hand,
Losing someone,
And sacrificing my career,
Only to be questioned,
"Who asked you to do that?"

I never thought I'd
Pick myself up again—
To conquer my insecurities,
Stand firm,
And know my worth.

It's an investment in myself—
The time, the love,
The understanding it took.

93

WE WIN IN THE END

Through trials,
I learned to climb back up again,
To pick my heart
From its shattered state,
To become empathetic.

I learned that not everyone comes to stay,
Not everything that shines is gold.

I learned that falling down is not a failure—
The failure lies in not trying to rise again.

Being cheated on is not a failure;
But you fail when you let yourself trust him again.

Failure comes when we refuse to accept and let go.
We fail ourselves and
The people who believe in us.

Trust me, all of us have given up
At one point.
Everybody has setbacks,
Heartbreaks.
What makes us whole is finding strength
While accepting vulnerability,
Unwilling to let go of ourselves.

We win.
We win in the end.

94

"I OWE AN APOLOGY TO MYSELF"

I owe myself an apology.
For staying even when I knew I wasn't needed,
Appreciated, respected, or loved.

I owe an apology for not standing up
For myself, for my rights.

I owe an apology for suppressing my inner voice,
For letting it be drowned out in silence.

Today, I owe an apology for every choice
That hurt me,
For every time I broke my own heart
And allowed others to do the same.

But I forgive myself,
For the things I did when I was immature,
For the times I didn't know any better.
I forgive to heal.
I forgive and love myself again.

95

TRUST YOUR WINGS

I was immature when I cried over the falls,
Now, I'm happy that they happened,
For what they showed me:
My strengths and vulnerabilities.

My dear ones who supported,
The pretenders,
The back giggles,
Showed real care.

The journey has shaped me—
From being scared,
Uncertain, willing to do anything
To not let go of that person,
To let go of anything
That doesn't serve me peace.

Like a baby bird, scared of its first flight,
Not knowing the strength
That lies in its wings.

I too was scared of
Uncertainty and feeling unloved,
But I learned I can't love anyone
Without loving myself first,
And self-love comes with a lot of goodbyes,
For the greater good to happen.

Don't be bothered by outer calamities,
Trust your wings.

96

"A JOURNEY THROUGH TIME"

I look back today,
And smile.
How far I've come—
From thinking life had ended,
To realizing life is just ahead.

How far I've come,
Living in fear,
When fear itself doesn't exist.

I understand now—
Fear is the unknown.

How far I've come,
No longer cursing myself
For the mistakes I made in haste,
When so little I knew.

How far I've come—
A four-year journey
That feels like lifetimes.

Wisdom took over,
And I healed.

97

"FROM PUPPY TO FIRE"

I was a people-pleaser,
A calm little puppy,
Loving, loyal,
Accepting everything
As love, disguised in darkness.

Gone are the days
When I lacked boundaries.
Gone are the times
I let silence speak for me.

Now, I burn bridges
And don't look back.
I walk away with strength,
Knowing I'm worth more
Than what was once given.

98

DREAM HOUSE

The dream house I bought,
Brought me a sense of satisfaction.
Looking at the large windows,
Reaching the sky,
I feel the yellow paint changing the vibe—
Making it feel happy.

I can sit on the sofa in the corner,
Staring at the sky until late at night.
From the windows that reach up to the sky,
I've proudly decorated the showcase
With all my framed certificates and awards.

Years of hard work paid off.
I can finally say,
I achieved the dreams I saw while awake.

99

"UNDER THE UNIVERSE'S EMBRACE"

I stood on the empty road,
Drenched in rain,
Watching everyone run,
Fearing the water's touch.

I stood on the empty road,
As dark clouds swallowed the sun,
Gripping the sky in their hold.

I stood on the empty road,
While the rain washed away my burdens,
Standing still, I felt relieved.

The whole universe was on my side,
An unseen aid,
Like a father who thunders
When his little one is hurt,
Like a mother wiping away tears,
Gently washing my face.

The universe held me in its embrace,
And I let it.

100

SEEKING PEACE

Be it age,
or the wisdom earned through struggle,
whatever it may be,
I seek peace—
peace within,
peace around.

I've learned to live in my zen,
unbothered by the chaos surrounding me.
With every experience I've had,
good or bad,
they are the stepping stones
that guide me toward serenity.
One day at a time,
I know tranquility awaits
at the end of this tunnel.

I remind myself to embrace each emotion as it comes—
only then can we heal.
Love, hate, betrayal, redemption, jealousy—
each feeling teaches me something valuable.
It's all about seeing through the lens of learning.

For every black, there's a white,
and for every white, there's a black.
Like yin and yang,
the balance of life unfolds.

101

HEALING ISN'T LONELY

My healing journey isn't lonely.
Many have contributed—
The smiles they passed as I walked by,
The small gestures of care,
Understanding my silence.

My dog helped me heal in the highest form,
The love she gave
Healed many versions of me.
The happiness I felt when I looked into her eyes,
Soothed my aching soul.

The tail wags when she saw me,
The slurry kisses,
Wanting to play,
When I was drowned,
She pulled me—
Pulled me out
With her naughtiness,
And a big wide smile.

Healing isn't done alone,
It's accompanied by the small actions—
Nature, pets, friends,
Strangers—
Helping us find our way.

ENDING NOTE

As I close the pages of this collection, I leave behind more than words. Each poem holds a fragment of my journey, a piece of my soul, shared with the hope that it resonated with yours. Yet, the path doesn't end here. In the quiet spaces between these lines, new stories are waiting to unfold. The heart that bleeds in these pages continues to seek, to love, to heal. And so, the pen keeps moving, crafting the philosophy of what lies ahead—the search for meaning, the unraveling of life's mysteries, and the questions that will always remain.

Stay with me, for the next chapter is already taking shape, where the echoes of love, loss, hope, and healing will find new verses to call home, and where the pursuit of deeper understanding will guide the poetry yet to come.

9 789369 549276

Printed by Libri Plureos GmbH in Hamburg,
Germany